I0830538

PEOPLE PROBLEMS

The Herd's Built-In Resistance to Genius

A KAREN KELLOCK PICTURESTRIP

PEOPLE PROBLEMS
The Herd's Built-In Resistance to Genius

Written and Illustrated by

Karen Kellock Ph.D.

Manual for Superior Men

A complete theory based on Einstein physics, Political Psychology, Systems Theory and Archetypal Psychiatry.

FORMULA

All success attraction
All disease obstruction
All recovery elimination

You must fast on all three

OBSTRUCTIONS:

People
Habit
Food

PEOPLE PROBLEMS

The dumber they are the more social! Think of that when they bug you to go but you don't want to.   If you wanna be alone that's when they'll invade. They get a little restless and wanna make you pay.   Instead of raging with frustration at the interruption learn to see it as a lesson: need more assertion.   It is not freeing or expanding to be social, it's more like a prison. Break out, be free, spirit is risen.

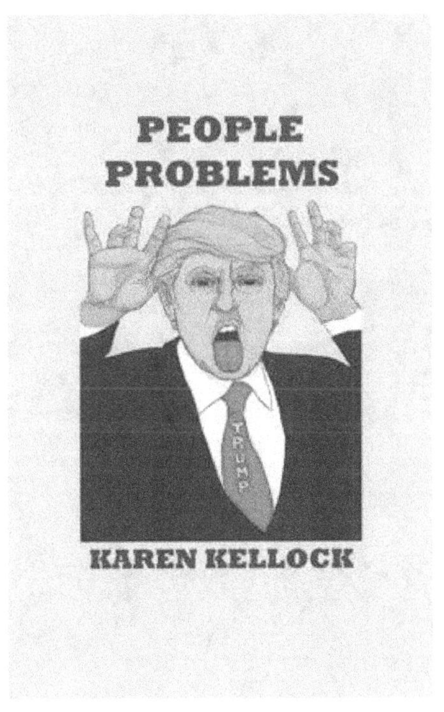

THEY WILL PERISH

DON'T HURT THE LITTLE PEPOLE
LET THEM GO FOR GOOD
THEY WANNA BE WITH WINNERS
GAIN FREEDOM FROM NO FRIENDS
UNFAIR COMPARISONS
CREATIVE FIRE FROM REJECTION
GO GREY ROCK, AT LEAST
HEALING POST NARC
HE'S NOT GROWING, YOU ARE
EXPECT THEM TO FEEL LONELY
SMASHING THRESHHOLD LEVELS
THEIR APOLOGY IS A LOVE BOMB
GET A LOYAL PARTNER
DON'T HANG ON TO PEOPLE
PRAY FOR A PARTITION
YOUR TRUE SELF EXHILARATES
FORGIVE TO BE FREE OF EM
THE SCAPEGOAT CAN DO NO RIGHT
SEXUAL WITCHCRAFT
NARCISSISTS NEED A DOORMAT
THEY ARE LAWLESS, BRAINLESS MORONS
THE CREATIVE ACT IS GIVING BIRTH
LET IT BE DONE, AND *OVER*
END THOUGHTS
GIVE EM A BREAK

THEY WILL PERISH

People are not that important, get that thru your head. Most are gonna perish/you've got goals instead.

Once finding out we don't hurt the little people but we don't get involved with em either: whew.

For the little people will hurt and let you down. Poor character doesn't even describe the dumbs.

Get good at saying goodbye and your whole destiny will open up. Keep old frenemies around and rust.

Once you go back you give em all the power to weaken you AGAIN. Never, ever let em back in son.

Don't trust people but rise up to lead the rabble for they need someone to bust their little bubbles.

Prepare: After being gutted emotionally and left flat you finally healed & now they want you back.

In the old days people courted and married. Now dating is sex see then dumping is hurried.

The rejection by/walking away from people can be the greatest time making you high as a steeple.

It was a DISMISSIVE discard--never forget that. They felt superior to you, don't neglect that fact.

DON'T HURT THE LITTLE PEPOLE

THEY WILL PERISH

When on top they'll all come back and flatter you up but isn't it a little late after how they screwed up?

Don't hurt the little people just see who they are and they'll fall away. Works every time, hurray.

Never talk to your neighbor again if she's just another jealous female for they're all alike ya' know.

The answer is to get lost in your work, spend every happy minute creatively and forget that jerk.

LET THEM GO FOR GOOD

If they wanna go, LET THEM GO. And do a door slam so they don't come back--now you're all aglow.

When these rebuffs happened when young I felt my gut turn over but never knew what it meant son.

It registers that you're inferior to them. Then it acts as a script: we act out that image from then on.

It'll never happen again, they can go to hell, that's your attitude. Hold your head up high dude.

Somehow the narcissist always ends up ruling.   They determine everything even the rejecting.

After draining your energy/charisma they dumped you but now you've recovered again they want you.

Use this most fertile time of rejection to flower into your creative best side: wait for the explosion!

For it's REJECTION that triggers the phoenix to rise from the dust, your TRUE SELF is finally coming up!

You hit the gym, get into new fashion, work on your finances increasin' and they'll want you again.

THEY WILL PERISH

If you stay dumb and let em back in you've had it man. But maybe you need to learn your lesson.

Don't let em back in. Life's too short for this gamin'. Be a queen or a king again, don't forget their sin.

Never break no-contact by getting the last word in. In the eyes of a narc that's weaselly vacillation.

I shot up like a rocket after breaking from that maggot who kicked me to the curb like a bad habit.

They're like one who gets rid of a dog then wants him back, shocked that it's too late, he's dead.

Don't forget their dismissive discard. How it gutted your soul/started a healing journey [hard].

And now they want you back: narcissists are always like that but too bad, leave them as sad sacks.

THEY WANNA BE WITH WINNERS

They wanna be on the winning team and not miss out--so what. Leave them flat and then spring up.

Narcissists are parasites: ugly barnacles veiled by a great act at first which turned to shit, yikes.

They want what you have but when exhausted from their presence you've nothing more to give.

You were the empath always doctoring their emotions until you lost attraction after drained by them.

Don't go back or waste more time and maybe not get up again, friend of mine. Open to victory, aye!

THEY WILL PERISH

In the narcissists way, they felt superior and thought nothing of dumping a replaceable inferior.

Don't go back, things always get worse. You've improved so you look better of course.

Pray God puts a partition between you and the pest. This works perfectly & permanently I attest.

You wasted time: you were actually working for the narcissist. Muse on this uneven relationship.

I saw self-improvement as the answer to rejection at age 12 when first boyfriend dumped this gal.

GAIN FREEDOM FROM NO FRIENDS

You must stop trusting humans entirely and give up on having friends too sweetie. Now you are FREE!

For inside YOU in cahoots with GOD there's enough power to solve any prob and give the rod.

For people bring disappointment and obstruction to all you want. Do it yourself and become BOSS.

Withdraw dependency on people & get your life back. Become a child again while ruling the flock dad.

No more being disappointed by people. Become boss and just fire their ass when you see the devil.

Be like Mother Theresa who saw people as naive little children who were evil and in need of motherin'.

UNFAIR COMPARISONS

THEY WILL PERISH

Lady: Withdraw from those who can't see your worth and who actually compare you to inferior girls.

Unfair comparisons hurt and degrade your worth. Stay away from those who are part of the world.

Be a queen/king. Don't chase earthlings but improve yourself to attract all that you're desiring.

As long as you're one of them you'll be abused. Gotta rise above em but you're already there Sue.

In dense generations they're all narcissists cuz they're all into self-defense, emotional survivalists.

After all you did for them as empath those ingrates dumped you for others, seeking greener paths.

CREATIVE FIRE FROM REJECTION

I pray you'll react to rejection with creative fire as I have. It's the only way and acts as a spiritual salve.

Don't talk to those people, they don't deserve you anymore. Heal from rejection, open to power.

Don't think back to your bootcamp, your Ph.D. in the Streets, your lessons about the creeps.

Once you've graduated, move on. Enjoy all the benefits of being alone above the crowd, prosperin'.

The narcissist made you an unpaid helper and walking apology. It will never be a healthy system see.

Narcissists live in a very narrow world they control and if you can't adapt to that you're repelled.

THEY WILL PERISH

The narc uses silent treatment as often as he can. You end up apologizing for nothing you did man.

You'll do anything to get his attention back since he talks to everyone else. That's the narcissist.

"I forgive thee" virtually means "get outa me" cuz that's what you're doing as the response to treachery.

To heal you must remove the narcissist, all flying monkeys and all other associates sis.

To heal you must cut out the whole cancer: extended relations who also went silent on her.

GO GREY ROCK, AT LEAST

Go greyrock on the silent treatment gag. Don't overshare/give bare minimum: it's a red flag.

You must also cut out all those believing the smear campaign of the narcissist: that's a must.

Breaking the trauma bond, exiting the devaluation stage and narcissistic fog: thank you God!

It was hell learning my biggest lesson: that most people don't have our best interests at heart son.

Rid of the narcissist your phoenix rises from the dust and from then on it's systems you resist.

Mastering your silence is a super power and amazing skill. Think of all the people who truckle.

HEALING POST NARC

THEY WILL PERISH

Healing in the post-narcissistic relationship brings amazing wholeness for the first time: bliss.

You devote that time as his helper to yourself and the results accrue showing amazing results.

HE'S NOT GROWING, YOU ARE

He's not growing, wasting time with a new supply that won't work out while you've grown way above.

You begin to work to not upset them, to avoid an uneasy vibe towards you. It's a mind screw.

This is how they eclipse your personality, the host: they maintain their reality by punishing novelty.

Block the narcissist, slow your life down, enjoy the silence. What a relief after so much offense.

They're trying to mold you into something that fits their psychic needs. It's not truth they seek.

You must fit their narrow world they have control over and never breach those limits sir.

After the discard the narcissist doesn't miss you but the supply you gave em: love/adoration/attention.

Stop letting em come in and out of your life when it's convenient to. Stop working for them Sue.

EXPECT THEM TO FEEL LONELY

After the discard the narcissist may feel lonely and reappear as if nothing's happened see.

THEY WILL PERISH

Narcissists are wired to be re-attracted to people they've discarded when doing well again.

How can we cultivate virtues with shallow socializing? It's best to have few friends while growing.

Say something she doesn't like and now she's the victim and you're the culprit--yikes!

Female narcs: the uncanny ability to become a victim suddenly just by you speaking candidly.

They **HATE** your direct speech. They want grey area hodgepodge they can manipulate see.

Let your yay be yay, and nay nay. Get outa that relationship or become indifferent ok.

The narc relationship is **SO ABUSIVE** that the recovery is the opposite as the True Self takes off.

SMASHING THRESHHOLD LEVELS

A universal thinker will shock the narrow female and the result is a smear campaign/system fail.

The modern female can't take any kind of novelty other than a current narrative she swallowed see.

A female genius has no female friends and what little trust she ends up with falls on men.

Suffering is a school and trauma is the teacher. It's a rocketship launcher to be rid of that lecher.

The only way to win with a narcissist is to disengage or keep a totally superficial relationship.

THEY WILL PERISH

Dumper's Remorse: when they realize no one can replace you in service to the narcissist.

Looking back can't change the past but it becomes a compulsion as if thinking we can, alas.

I got so fed up with people I escaped into the right brain and have been there ever since ok.

I realized that doing my own thing felt a lot better than ever again being under their influence, ever.

If we don't chase the rejector eventually they're stuck with dumper's remorse, a real bummer.

THEIR APOLOGY IS A LOVE BOMB

Their apology is just a love bomb. They don't miss you but the supply so just do a door slam mom!

They miss you but it's not YOU just supply coming through so ignore their dumper's remorse too.

Tho' ready for his predictable discard it scolded my soul anyway: don't play around with it ok.

Since she maintained her reality by punishing novelty I became really jittery fearing offending see.

GET A LOYAL PARTNER

Hopefully by now you have one loyal partner and have survived people problems: what a vacation.

THEY WILL PERISH

You have learned to LET EM GO and perfected the Art of Goodbye. You vet your associates well, aye.

For people are the Number One Obstruction. Eliminate them and get ready for a giant reward, amen.

They tainted your soul and degraded your self-esteem. They start out good then get snippy subtly.

DON'T HANG ON TO PEOPLE

By hanging onto people for reassurance we lose good breaks and new chances. Let em go, progress.

They're like barnacles on a ship that weaken it. They drag you down tho' much is inadvertent.

They subtly tho' politely showed their disdain for your ideas. It's an insult but you stayed sis.

I gave birth to a marvelous work and wonder and I don't know why God chose me as the vessel sir.

God chose the exceptionally energetic who stays up all night to do a work of great complexity, aye.

You feel to end the bad relationship means death but really it's a whole new beautiful life instead.

PRAY FOR A PARTITION

Ask for God's help and He'll build a partition between you and the questionable character son.

God will show when he wants a relationship to end. We come in alone and go out that way friend.

THEY WILL PERISH

Alone, you're the perfect diamond but with inappropriate others you become faded out.

Your relief in the face of karmic justice brings a feeling of exhilaration--it's how it's supposed to be son.

JUSTICE is necessary for the relief of the saints. It's an attribute of God and thus brings happiness.

Not only do they get theirs, they have to witness the banquet God puts on for you afterwards.

Satan is arrogant and they felt better than you. They thought nothing of discarding such a fool.

Narcissists don't think things thru Sue and reject without any explanation nor closure too.

YOUR TRUE SELF EXHILARATES

It was exhilarating as the True Self swung forward, kept dormant by being constantly devalued.

It's the story of human nature since relationships are basic to it. It can be lethal so God wants in it.

Future faking is none more than an empty transaction. In great detail they promise you everything.

When you say "I forgive you" see it as meaning "get outa me now" as you're now free of a black cloud.

FORGIVE TO BE FREE OF EM

The golden child can do no wrong and blame you for everything then they collude with the mom.

THEY WILL PERISH

So long as you stay mad at them they're IN YOU like a trash bin. Forgive to be FREE of them son.

THE SCAPEGOAT CAN DO NO RIGHT

The scapegoat can do no right and when golden child teams with mom you're up a creek, aye.

Face it: the drunkard's your worst enemy wanting nothing more than to see you dead honey.

The golden child could do anything and laugh in your face. The narcissistic system is a disgrace.

The golden child and mom blame the scapegoat for everything conceivable that's gone wrong.

Mom and golden child are same dark energy cycle but through their virtue signaling it's all veiled.

The scapegoat puts in the search: "sister hates me" and the info changes life suddenly/removes curse.

Information will nullify the stings of the narcissist or his plans to keep you down and distressed.

A scapegoat puts in the search: "sister hates me" and info removes the curse/changes life suddenly.

You've reached the mountaintop of indifference: only it will save you from that lying nuisance.

Saying YES would disregulate me immediately. That's what happens to traumatized nerdies.

Modern trends degrade women. It's part of the backlash of feminism: get on your knees-ism.

THEY WILL PERISH

SEXUAL WITCHCRAFT

It's how to get a husband but deny it afterwards: oral sex is witchcraft/both sexes manipulators.

Both sexes use carnal witchcraft as bartering tools/means of manipulation: SEE this you fools!

Saying YES to any social event would bring thoughts of how I'm gonna get out of it. Disregulation

What exacerbates symptoms: age and degree of trauma. I just can't take it anymore momma.

Blocking em ends the indecision. Back and forth, up and down and it's all blather & shady dealins'.

A CROWD DRIVES GENIUS MAD

A crowd drives the hypersensitive extreme ectomorph wild but is nothing to a socialized child.

A reclusive hyperevolute empath cerebrotonoic preferring privacy: that's all I want see.

Just shut the fruit up is what I say to anyone entering my den cuz nothing compares to it friend.

Alone I enter 1000 universes/inner rooms all with the sign "enter here, not a tear"/full of splendor.

And then someone interrupts with small talk/trivia, wondering why I don't want them in the area.

They get supply from you being miserable but if you're doing well they don't wanna let that go.

THEY WILL PERISH

Forgive yourself for being a fool and prepare yourself for letting it all go too: 2 things you gotta do.

NARCISSISTS NEED A DOORMAT

A narcissist needs a doormat who has low self-esteem, lacks confidence and is codependent.

You think "wow, maybe this could work" then here it comes again: gaslit, stonewalled, cursed.

It's too easy to take things out on a clerk. Think things thru before going crazy/acting like a jerk.

People are cruel so genius stays clear. You've got to if wanting to accomplish things/be a seer.

They hated me too. I was the scapegoat and sis was golden child colluding with the narc mom.

Better to wait a little longer than to go out before you're ready--and then it's indelible for eternity.

Start the weekend right now, that means no more work. You're OFF--into the right brain of course.

I recall a past as nothingness peppered with bad events but now each day is big even the moments.

I won't be here forever, I'm getting closer to the end sir but each day is magnified in how I see her.

If you live 25 more years its 300 months, 1300 weeks or 9100 days: no matter your age be prolific ok.

What 75 year old thinks like that? More likely they're preparing for the grave, gone and flat.

THEY WILL PERISH

Every theory has a formula and this is about elimination: you gotta get rid of her/him.

The thing is: they felt superior to you at the time so cast you aside--but you grew, now they cry.

A happy home is heaven but a dysfunctional warring home is hell on earth & nothing ever forgiven.

The fastest way to prosperity is to trust God. Stay clear of worthless accomplishments/the flawed.

Can't read, write or do math, can't see a difference between right and wrong: that's the mass.

THEY ARE LAWLESS, BRAINLESS MORONS

They are lawless, brainless morons, an army of idiots: the result of government schools: see it.

Before government got involved with education you had 100% literacy & people were smarter see.

They actually made us think socializing was more important than doing math or writing.

There are decades when nothing's happening and weeks when decades are happening.

Both our youth and the migrants have been taught to hate America so good luck to all of ya'.

THE CREATIVE ACT IS GIVING BIRTH

The Creative Act is like giving birth: Coming up to the event is labor then afterwards it's over.

THEY WILL PERISH

Eras of maudlin self-dejection & cryin' always precedes a giant explosion like creative rebrandin'.

It's done, you've completed your assignment. You gotta know it's done [& backed up] to enjoy it.

LET IT BE DONE, AND *OVER*

It's done, and it's over. I've given birth to the Creative Act and now I can retire for thirty years.

The suffering going into it was endured when young, the work load when mature and now it's over.

I couldn't go on with this level of complexity, it completed right when I felt a little crazy.

Retirement: phase of adventure. It's enjoying the fruits of your labor, by now you have God's favor.

END THOUGHTS

Little weasels talking of "stopping Trump" when things were never better, now we're a dam dump.

Donald Trump is the only bastion to protect us from an out of control left-wing government.

The difference between a democracy and a republic: the rule of law or the rule of the mob.

In a republic even if you have a tyranny of the majority you're still protected by a bill of rights see.

Trump's got a list ready of 30,000 unelected posts filled by MAGA patriots for when he's boss.

THEY WILL PERISH

Leave your antisemitic liberal/college friends behind and join the ranks of the elect/truly refined.

When busy/stressed it saves time to go into a fast. Endure a couple hunger pains then have a blast.

I get too busy to eat, to fix something. It's just much easier to fast then succeed at everything.

GIVE EM A BREAK

Give em a break: go beyond macaroni and cheese. Geez, get a little creative won't you please.

Tacos or pizza with lowcarb tortilla or bacon and eggs will serve ya'. Really, what else is there?

Now I'll make videos I guess tho' I hate being seen. Shyness is something to be gotten over see.

I prefer wool cashmere sweaters, they just feel better but I hate what woolies goes thru however.

Don't make a big deal of it, just write it in a book. Your experiences are invaluable for the group.

Stuff in info from the outside but then let it percolate with music as you relate it to your insides.

PEOPLE IN THEIR SYSTEMS

RELAXING INTO NO SELF-PROTECTION
REGRESSION INTO LA LA LAND
NEED TO PLEASE
STRONG INNER CRITIC
OPEN ATTACHMENT SYSTEM
GETTING HOOKED BY LUNATICS
TEACH THE EMPATH THIS
YOUR MIND IS A BATTLEFIELD
HERE STARTS THE NARC STRUCTURE
BROKEN HEART, CRUSHED SPIRIT
DON'T HOLD ONTO THE DEAD
RECLAIM YOUR SOUL FROM NARCISSISTS
A FIGHT FOR YOUR LIFE
ONLY YOU CAN ORDER YOUR MIND
TRIANGULATIONS AND COMPARISONS
TME PROTECTED MATURE EMPATH
WITH THE CHILD INTEGRATED

PEOPLE IN THEIR SYSTEMS

It is the vacillations between idealizing and discarding that keep you sick in this relationship.

Why do empaths cave in to lovebombing or idealization? A hyper-activated attachment system.

Agreeableness/poor assertion/need to please shows an underdeveloped warrior/defense system.

Her Internal Warrior was missing while she made herself sick with no defense against hicks.

The empath's internal critic is the introjection of all negative messages received from the system.

This especially strong internal critic thwarts their self-awareness or ability to see their condition.

Her core systems [agreeableness, poor assertion and need to please] are highjacked by narcissist.

Give God tools--no contact, no lurking/online stalking, do your own thing--and He removes fools.

RELAXING INTO NO SELF-PROTECTION

During lovebombing it's an hyper-activated system as the narcissist mirrors her deepest emotions.

As he lavishes excessive praise and attention onto the empath she laps it up tho' its unrealistic slop.

PEOPLE IN THEIR SYSTEMS

Empath thinks "this is unreal" [as someone actually values her for who she is] but it's temporary bliss.

He says "you're perfect, best thing ever happening to me": so she lets down on need to please.

Her internal critic is also relaxed since his love bombing replaces the original bully's image-bash.

All of her sense of unworthiness is squashed by his incessant, inordinate attention--soon lost.

Her compulsive need to give/please is relaxed [for she is enough] as she senses her own needs.

You didn't hurt me by doing that. You showed me who you are, a dirty rat, and I was glad at that.

As she relaxes her core systems she regresses into infantilization with no self-protection.

Just as she's seduced into the idea of complete symbiotic union he'll pull the rug out too.

REGRESSION INTO LA LA LAND

In initial stages she regressed into an infantile state as if returning to the bosom of the mother ok.

All of their needs will be met/their worries taken care of: that's the message to the naive empaths.

People can get you into a world of trouble if you don't stay on top of things/check it all out see.

She falls asleep at the wheel until the rug's pulled out suddenly and she's just another dam fool.

Reframing or making light of inconsistencies due to the bombardment of attention/approval getting.

NEED TO PLEASE
STRONG INNER CRITIC
OPEN ATTACHMENT SYSTEM

Note how these underlying elements in one's personality structure makes them vulnerable forever.

Empaths need authentic connection to themselves and THEIR own needs to be free and happy.

Empaths must develop critical self-awareness into their own dynamics or get hooked by lunatics.

To hell with the hostess thing, I wanted to be ALONE cuz that's when I'm happy/creativity-prone.

To heck with society, I didn't wanna be pressured to socialize or go anywhere and about status I don't even care.

He's been depedestalized, that's all I know guys. Thru prayer I'm finally free/he's nothing see, aye!

Why'd it take a lifetime to learn about ME? Woulda saved me infinite time for creativity.

But instead, due to early trauma my attachment system was easily opened and I'd get taken.

GETTING HOOKED BY LUNATICS

I got hooked by one lunatic after another, I honestly didn't know any better and mom didn't offer.

Along with her needs she must recognize the VOICE of her inner critic and get distance from it.

As an empath I had to develop my Inner Warrior to alert me to dysfunctional people wearing a smile.

PEOPLE IN THEIR SYSTEMS

Conflicted, pathological personalities are clearly averted by dogs and cats but not us empaths.

Due to low self-esteem and an open attachment system she got distracted by greener pastures again.

TEACH THE EMPATH THIS

The narcissist triggers these three systems to hardwire the bond so he takes control from then on.

Teach the empath how serious a life change can occur by getting involved with psycho pit vipers.

You can lose your life in a minute from the wrong association: stay in the divine groove, amen.

Never let flattery relax your vigilance. People: the main obstruction to mental health/intelligence.

People get us off our path. Through aggressive pressure and repetition we go along with psychopaths.

You wanna stay home and study, they pressure you to go out to the party. Pressure/judgment see.

There's a deep-seated belief in their unworthiness and unlovability, thus they're open to flattery.

Don't confront a narcissist about what you know, he's empty inside. Just learn about him and abide.

Most people will only subtract from you not add. We always think they will but there's a drag.

YOUR MIND IS A BATTLEFIELD

For the mind is a battlefield between good and evil and gets all tied up with the drama of people.

PEOPLE IN THEIR SYSTEMS

When God gives you rescue/a new life don't spit in His face with bad memories: control the mind.

Life is a pie: don't ruin divine present with thoughts of the past, your lesson. Make it lessen.

HERE STARTS THE NARC STRUCTURE

If spontaneous self-expression means humiliated, rejected or ignored here starts narc structure.

A narcissist parent is easily taken off track by the child's self-expression, so here it all started son.

The message: I don't care what you think and feel or your vulnerabilities, they make me anxious.

The child doesn't get accurate mirroring of his internal state, it's all about what parent wants ok.

The result is a child repeatedly put down in the expression of himself: invalidated/crushed.

The child's natural self-expression is stifled in exchange for what the parent demands or asks for.

Extension of themselves: the child is not seen for who they are but what they can do for parents.

In non-narcissism there's a sense of awe, wonder and unconditional positive regard for the infant.

Attachment is biologically hardwired to form bonds with our primary caregivers, esp. mother.

Masculine women preferring even meaner men? That's the trend, to get that magnetism goin'.

BROKEN HEART, CRUSHED SPIRIT

PEOPLE IN THEIR SYSTEMS

We can't begin to heal a crushed heart until we first understand the incomparable pain.

The pain of trauma/being broken emotionally cannot be compared to anything else in psychology.

The pain is felt randomly. Sometimes trauma is stored as feelings not memories--sporadically.

Our mood goes from exhilarating highs to dangerous lows due to trauma stored as feelings.

Hold onto the pain of something that's dead and done or feel the pain from letting go and run.

DON'T HOLD ONTO THE DEAD

Hold onto the dead and done and it costs you your life and destiny, your hard-won future finally.

Let future possibilities absorb you up into a white cloud, but not if still hung up on that guy so loud.

Envision a big balloon whisking you up and away, a magic carpet ride as you cut him loose ok.

Holding onto dead & done hoping for a revitalization of the thing rather than being done totally.

Let God be your First Love as He pulls you up and away from your crushed heart and this ingrate.

Thinking you need this person is worshipping the created not the Creator, your Rescuer.

Face the pain of letting go while you heal. Nothing good comes from holding onto the dead/unreal.

The pain is necessary in helping you renew your mind. No professor can do the same, aye.

PEOPLE IN THEIR SYSTEMS

The pain is necessary. You're choosing between two pains: it's just gotta be/you need to feel it.

Usually the pain delivers the lesson. Out of pain comes divine nectar of evolution and progression.

It is good for me that I have been afflicted that I might learn God's laws. Psalms 119: 71

You're gonna have to regulate your obsessive thoughts. You get stuck like a record, and stuck...

You put your mind in order, no one else. It's just you and God so YOU must do it, wipe it off.

RECLAIM YOUR SOUL FROM NARCISSISTS

Reclaim your soul from narcissist with humility and reason--from demons of hell/season of treason.

Broken consciousness focuses on the good times not the hell he put you thru with jails and lies.

Along with nostalgic happy memories is self-blaming, keeping one in the system/no complaining.

When your soul's been crushed by someone it's a battle for your life: spiritual wickedness, strife.

He's incomprehensibly boring but you find him fascinating due to the adrenalin-triggering.

A queen has a conflict, meets it with self-improvement and always comes out on top/totally legit.

A queen must always come out on top so improves a lot if that's whats needed to overcome a nut.

I go to God, my Father, and humbly ask him to overcome this matter, totally trampling it under.

PEOPLE IN THEIR SYSTEMS

Like someone's superiorizing over me, that's enough to bring His wrath as proven often in the past.

A FIGHT FOR YOUR LIFE

Becoming emotionally invulnerable, that is the goal. Let em rant and rave, you stay stoic/stable.

Exit all situations where you're compared with grunts: you're the cat's meow/they're just fronts.

Spiritual wickedness in high places is why it's hard to release a narcissist but with God we must.

Through knowledge he's been dethroned in your eyes and that's all that matters at this vital time.

Never let em know what you know/your exit strategy. As an ex-escapee I warn you: keep SECRECY.

Even if it's an internet thing you still need escape as if he's in the room. No lurking: I'm telling you.

You need to transcend this person totally for he's eclipsed your entire personality, oh my...

ONLY YOU CAN ORDER YOUR MIND

YOU need to save your soul/order your mind from [high place wickedness] a fight for your life.

The narcissist is envious and vindictive: walk away gently with no desire to show off/get back.

A fight for your life: don't sink in your swill, leak self-esteem or apologize to the creep, abide.

Why is it so hard to release it? It's spiritual--demonic. You must be strong and go No Contact.

PEOPLE IN THEIR SYSTEMS

Many women wanna intermingle with the man who hurt em and wonder why they're stuck/down.

To beat cocaine addiction you don't keep lines on your table. You gotta go no contact/that's FINAL.

You gotta renew your mind: forcefully manage your own thought life. Block him out, it's only strife.

As you stay in this battle your heart gets healthier every day. You've been held down ruthlessly.

TRIANGULATIONS AND COMPARISONS

It is the comparisons with mediocre nobodies that makes you feel like s**t down in the pits.

You must face the mindless delusion you've been caught in--thinking he was actually open.

To heal a crushed heart live just for the best version of you. Not just being sorry/you must eschew.

You've been living your life for him/them. Now it's time to live it for you and to hell with them.

There's no healing without turning. Turn from your wicked ways then hear from heaven surely.

God said He'd even heal our land if we turn from our sin which in your case was a person/a man.

Not enough to be "sorry'--to repent means to TURN FROM to be in line with God's will, today.

It's a healing process--you'll be going thru CYCLES. The downswings are painful, they pass tho'.

TME PROTECTED MATURE EMPATH

PEOPLE IN THEIR SYSTEMS

You don't see yourself as edging into obsolesce, you're preparing for your last hurrah, in silence.

Edging into obsolescence or far more mature self-awareness shrewdly staying behind a fence?

She lost touch with her own critical faculties and falls asleep to her own intuition/gut knowing.

She needs to get self-awareness about protection vs pathology to keep these kinds of guys away.

The mature empath unites with inner child and becomes energized as a new person/self-styled.

WITH THE CHILD INTEGRATED

No longer split, he's energized by an entirely different view of self and that's the mature empath.

The narcissist could only access us thru the inner child without protection but that's fixed now, done.

The compact between adult and child is restored as now the child's protected from toxic users.

The mature child is free now to express it's life essence without fear, maybe even a famous seer.

United with child the adult matures beyond it's specific woundings which limits it's knowings.

Our personal story and wounds blocks us from a healing more transcendent identity beyond us.

Both naive innocence and cynical hardheartedness are overtaken by this new mature perspective.

Having transcended their own ego narrative, their wounding, they're invulnerable to deceiving.

PEOPLE IN THEIR SYSTEMS

Healing this empath-narcissist dynamic ultimately needs a holistic and spiritual view on it.

An adult with a healed & integrated inner child with true warrior energy AND linked to God: wow!

PEOPLE PROBLEMS 1
The Herd's Built-In Resistance to Genius

If you're a thinker or tinkerer, you gotta manage people. You have hours, protectors, locked doors.

Loyalty to the group must transcend autonomy but I couldn't do that you see: I wanted my liberty.

That I'd rather stay home alone than go to a social was just too much to those without goals.

Every time I went out I wished I'd stayed home. I just never left paradise again, never to roam.

Nothing out there can compare with life in here. If only women knew this life would seem fair.

Success is not from east or west but from God who puts one down as he makes the other renowned.

Prepare to come out of obscurity. I know it's like a blanket of cozy security, being holed in constantly.

Social is the whole thing--as it degrades so too their corny personalities and true genius is a rarity.

I will never be in that rejecting matrix again. I'm out of it and don't care if you're my friend.

They think they are so funny but entirely corny cuz they cheer each other on in their own reality.

PEOPLE PROBLEMS

If you're alone God has singled you out for a job and doesn't want other influences messing it up.

I wanna stay home with the wind and my pets. Not smile and laugh, answer questions/deal with pests.

I went thru terrible things to learn the lesson: build a high wall or this day you won't be enjoyin'

Husband loves it too: High walls, locked gate. He says in amazement: "I never felt this way!"

Life has shocks and betrayals when it all goes upside down. In an instant we go humble from renowned.

You have enemies? Good--that means you stood up for something. Winston Churchhill

In the end we will remember not the words of our enemies but the silence of our friends. M.L. King

Think of their insult. Don't drink or eat it down, face it. Now overcome the crazy nuts and make it.

Now's the time to think ahead: success--outa old systems keeping you down/creating a mess.

There were no lost years as underneath something was brewing that went way beyond tears.

Payback is your success. God promised it after you planted the seed to transcend this mess.

Payback is something you gotta see--you never did one darn thing for me and now we're family?

PEOPLE PROBLEMS

He acts so nice then tosses you a zinger, one that takes forever to get over.

I couldn't understand those who knew everyone's name and number while I lived in an ivory tower.

I felt invaded by everyone, it seemed I never had time alone. They'd get angry cuz time was my own.

The new age hates those with convictions and goals cuz it makes them feel less, that's taboo.

You fear going out there tho' that is your role. Give this to God, He'll see you through/console.

Just work in the morning then spend all day getting ready for the next morning, you'll be soaring.

Man, you were just my springboard to a higher life--my reward after going through so much strife!

The value of privacy is not realized until it is lost.

Regimen: Work from 3 - 8 am. Rest of the day get high (receptive) for next morning preparation.

These quips are whatcha call "essentially true".

Deceitful relationships bring gut aches constantly then other people hop on adding fuel to your misery.

Solar plexus is felt in gut--it tells you there's discordance in your environment, you're in a rut.

You're in denial but your solar plexus (GUT) isn't and it may explain your headaches too: listen.

PEOPLE PROBLEMS

Frenemies are usurpers and foes and it's even in your family, you know. It's this era/wish it weren't so.

Denial--a safety mechanism for survival?

To forgive, go back into denial and live.

If you are not rehorrified at the ridiculous you'll be resavaged in adapting to that environment worse.

The day and hour of world success cannot be predicted but can be anytime since the work is done.

Every sentence is saying the same thing in a different way.

I've done all I can, wrote a 1400 page book about how crazy they are. Now I'll retire/you do your part.

Don't pain for those who left you: use it for your success and going ahead-- don't you want that?

Think of their insult. Now use that to galvanize energy for improvement and total success, do it.

Befriend my foe, you're out the door.

Prejudice. Use the insult to galvanize energy for total success and never see them again.

You win and rule cuz you know how to do things best. Resisted all the way, finally you're the head.

Do your work/pray = way ahead of the game.

If you feel it speak it cuz you're speaking to us all--we went through it all too: LIFT US:

PEOPLE PROBLEMS

The dumber they are the more social! Think of that when they bug you to go but you don't want to.

I escaped the social mazeway of a small desert town by moving way out, then real lessons began.

I learned to love my cabin in the wilderness, my waterloo, my nemesis for what I'd been through.

Lessons were about boundaries and assertion: Don't come here, get out: that was my education.

I was invaded by thugs and police wouldn't protect me--that's just like now, it's a world tragedy.

If you've got liberal characteristics I'm gonna see it.

You should release with love but sometimes you first gotta release with hate, but do it anyway.

I'm thru feeling rejected by you so I release you now and that's like a big Christmas present too.

Build your fence before they make it illegal, like Houston. Can you believe that--they want us down.

Although there are brilliant thinkers like me most women are stark raving mad, they just can't see.

If you wanna be alone that's when they'll invade. They get a little restless and wanna make you pay.

Instead of raging with frustration at the interruption learn to see it as a lesson: need more assertion.

PEOPLE PROBLEMS

If you feel inspired, if God's given you an assignment, you must detach--that's your achievement.

It is not freeing or expanding to be social, it's more like a prison. Break out, be free, spirit is risen.

Separate/solitude = sanctified/holy.

It's especially hard for female genius since solitude is a hideous stigma in this generation I guess.

A captured soul collapses in Stockholm Syndrome then can't say "no" and is taken completely over.

Lack of assertion or boundaries means evil flows in and you're either dead or a life failure instead.

People can't do more than their genetically programmed to and if you correct they'll get mad too.

They can't see it, period. It's outa their frame of reference so open up to another or you'll be out of it.

You're asking for delicacy, tact, refinement--they don't have it and never will. It's genes, get real.

85% of communication is non-verbal so don't listen to words, read body language signs if you're able.

You're asking legless men to run a race. They just can't do it, they don't care and it's best to escape.

Repartee: Adroitness and cleverness in reply.

PEOPLE PROBLEMS

Fallen Hero Syndrome: everyone jumps on the bandwagon to bring him down, that's the human pound.

God said: Stop adding fuel to the fire and I'll erase this right now.

For there shall be no reward for the evil man; the lamp of the wicked shall be put out. Prov 24: 20

Do not associate with those who are given to change or allegiance. Prov. 24: 21.

Take away the wicked before the king, and his throne will be established in righteousness Prov 24: 25.

Your problem is trying to sell yourself rather than doing something great.

I'll never let you uglify my surroundings again.

A poet is an ocean of emotion so when things go wrong it's a Tsunami: watch out, much commotion.

Attitude is great but how can you have one if you don't know what the heck you're talkin' about?

Virtue signaling marks the liberal--that's how we know.

Shut up with your attitude thing, making a fool of yourself spouting off like you know everything.

Born clear, we mal-adapt to an insane world and become dense. Seen that way it all makes sense.

I just spoke the truth as I saw it at that moment. Can't even remember what it was, I just trust it.

PEOPLE PROBLEMS

Adults are a haunted house as early traumas determine perception and I'd hate to be their victim.

You can't have personality without knowledge to pull it off. Build your identity/style, know your stuff.

Things happen, who can explain em, just trust Him.

A series of severe shocks then she changed the locks and returned to her own reality which rocks.

You don't have to give into demands. Stand your ground against the spirit of the communists.

All the glory goes to God because it's Him coming thru but you'll get all the worldly credit and soon.

I went thru dark slums/scary people/had burdens in learning scruples but the reward's so cool.

The Creative Act is a literal structure in nature, with a beginning and an end. Like a diamond.

You will know when you're done, but Einstein said "you cannot ever know until that point it's done."

We built a home together and it began by escaping California.

Forgive yourself for the demons with whom you kept company.

Forgive, forget and never speak of it again. Because of Jesus it doesn't exist, He erased the sin.

If He came thru the Creative Act He'll also smooth it out. He'll send His angels so let out a shout!

PEOPLE PROBLEMS

You've worked all your life, you've overcome so much. Now you've arrived and are remunerated, a bunch.

Keep on envisioning, creating, solving, overcoming, building and your time will come if you faint not.

It's archetypal: pre-success crises.

Einstein just woke up in fame. He'd worked all his life but it seemed overnight his world had changed.

Your remorse over eras when you were controlled by the devil: It's erased along with all evil.

Stop making up your own religion.

I couldn't live in town, it had to be nature so what could I do but take an existing shack, a humbler.

Let the reward be appreciation for what you've already been given.

Ok, so you don't wanna work. I can understand that, bye.

So take a million selfies you narcissist--abusing modern science for your boring self-indulgence.

You've had it up to here! Now's the time for delicious life change way ahead by light years.

It's not stuff/temporary events! They're over/gone then you're depressed? It's eternity you nuts.

Nothing feels so good as enantiodromia: system inversions where those on bottom now rule ya.

PEOPLE PROBLEMS

Ignore looks, status, time spent. Superficials are the devil's devices unworthy of God's attention.

The great thinkers become philosophers or die in the gutter as rejected and scorned failures.

How can a thinker or poet adapt to that? Nothing makes any sense so they just get drugged up.

The greatest saints were the worst sinners cuz they learned most from their mistakes and the Savior.

As horrible as it was, God was with me and He didn't give me more than I could take, but it sure took.

Just one little thing: if you take the ball and run with it, eternity, blessings, no more stressing.

She didn't get it, as usual it's the wrong emphasis.

It's your fault and they're good. What else to think when they're all the same, but it's social hypnotism.

Now we need protection from others. Fortunately we love our neighbors and they love us.

It's too late for them and life is short. You gotta get on with it and then you can make your mark.

We tend to get attached--but it's turns sick. Put your focus back on God and everything is fixed.

It's always been this way, hon': God's men stuck on the periphery until their time has come.

PEOPLE PROBLEMS

Everyone looks down on the superior men but success is reward for overcoming the challenge.

Don't you want that: to show the creepy haters who said it couldn't be done and see them go splat?

The only thing is: if an individual lover of truth you'll be alone but will learn to love going SOLO.

GO SOLO. So long, so low: I thought you had it all but wrong, just another bore in the throng.

God's timing: It's a day, hour and minute. Before that split second you're an unknown, even hated.

You have a rare knack no one else has. Human genius has infinite variety cuz God loves just us.

Push those creepy snobs outa your head cuz they don't pay rent there and never saw you as rare.

They've caused you aggravation so now stop your premature aging as God restores youth again.

The devil's crowd will always hold you down and you're outa grace cuz it's not where you belong.

God's done so much, forget those who blocked/creeped you out--they're only human/focus on God.

Those getting huffy at correction will make big mistakes requiring exaction.

Now let's go back to your household: the real queen is never seen but subtly sets the scene.

Don't try to make them see for they will never see. Just see them then realign to stay free.

PEOPLE PROBLEMS

Just cuz they say they can do the job doesn't mean they can so trust your guts not what is said.

Don't try to explain why trust is lost, just get away. These are now your enemies and they're not ok.

She got huffy with correction then proceeded to make the same mistake again. Predictable, huh

Where truth is gone it's all an outward show. Being nice, saying the right things, being aglow.

Huffy over correction, made mistake again.

Can't yell at the incompetent, all you can do is see them then re-align to maintain your freedom.

Stop giving importance to people yet never thinking of God. This is false religion: people-worshippin'

It's scary as ego alien material arises from collective unconscious but Jesus saves us from this.

Stop. Ponder. Don't compulse, focus.

Suddenly, in the twinkling of an eye, you'll meet the link to all the connections you'll need.

Don't compulse, you'll meet him in an elevator or other coincidence so: relax after great diligence.

Who cares--put em all in a bag to go out. Look at all their pics, put em in a folder, delete, shout.

Stop explaining yourself, it's a sign of weakness. It's them who explain themselves to you, or else.

PEOPLE PROBLEMS

Attachments (even through hate) are clouding your image which is destiny, fate, predesigned genius.

Cult of fame and red carpet lame. It's sickening to see your own kin display silly narcissist games.

The lowminded take 1000 pictures of themselves and it's death by a thousand cuts as wisdom falls.

For success, control your mind. No tangents or resentments and work things out before night.

Who cares what they think? They're insane or wouldn't have been attracted to you then, a fink.

Don't ever think of em, they're in the trash/recycle bin.

Forget em, they didn't want you. Think on that, let it make you great through and through.

I'm an isolate, don't like being seen but it's about the copy not me.

Hold back strength, don't work, listen to music/party as you wait for perks as leisure inspires works.

Breakups: They didn't want you--that's reason enough to never think of em again, now stop it.

They're just people, get over it. Love God He is preeminent.

They clearly thought no one was going to know/they could get away with it.

It doesn't matter what they think only what God thinks.

You can control him you just can't let him know.

PEOPLE PROBLEMS

Get some class. Take ONE picture of yourself, picking the best.

The social game: take pictures of yourself smiling like you're having the party of your life, beguiling.

Assemble a duffle of quintessential: most essential of all, to be ready to move when hearing the call.

Wipe that smirk off your face. Life is serious and you gotta ace. Focus, think of us, state your case.

The reason you should be serious/focused is trouble may come. No jocularity or running around.

Don't bemoan being alone cuz that's how you got so good and knowin'

Never let em frame you, frame yourself cuz true friends are few.

It is so dark, so frustrating--but likely part of the process: pre-success crisis.

Suddenly they see how empty they are. The ontologically fatal insight: it was all an illusion, bizarre.

Compromised Christians seek to be nice/not step on toes--weaklings unfit for the kingdom, foes.

Since they don't read the bible they think it's about social, hospitable, nice, with many friends.

Just cuz things aren't happening this minute, they panic. Learn patience: let it fall into a fabric.

You've had nothing but trouble so it's what you still expect-- but things will be easy now as God's Elect.

PEOPLE PROBLEMS

Only the smart can see the value. They're rare now so don't get down cuz everyone's so shallow.

You prayed, asked God to dissolve the block and got with brethren so now relax as it all fills in.

You must realize your potential while here on earth so don't waste a minute with framers/be alert.

Framers of your identity--either from past systems or ideology--will block your genius destiny.

There's no possible way for your joy with that going on in your home and I think you know that hon'

You can't be around that sort of thing even if it is your own kin. No boyfriends, locked doors, sin.

You had your chance backstabber it's called the big payback so go ahead with smiling and chatter.

This isn't the fifties, gone is all decency. But under my roof? No way missy

Parents afraid of putting their foot down, fear of insults all around? Now's the time to be strong!

Don't ever give up, where there's will there's a way, your faith is just being tested on this rainy day.

Things seem so bad you wanna end it all. Looks bleak but then prayer brings light/ends the stall.

The defining characteristic of anorexia is a wish to die. Jill Holm-Denoma

It is genetic and the symptoms roll out with stress as it does with all genetic illnesses.

PEOPLE PROBLEMS

Just wait for the link. God has it planned but waiting for that moment it may stink/you need a shrink.

Some women don't mind weight gain even big as a house, others may panic over a few pounds.

Man adapts to his environment like all animals. If it's sick and mixed up, it'd be a miracle to be on top.

What is maturity? It is unpeeling the cultural neurosis making us all crazy.

Sold me out, put me in chains. You had it all arranged, you handed me over, I felt so betrayed.

Took my money, got my honey, didn't want me to see what you're doing to me, payback not funny.

So let me get this: You're impressed with their outward success so can ignore the mess I guess?

Lives filled with correspondence, but is that all there is? No inner journey or sense of coincidence

In the old frontier, life was hard and often hideous. Danger being imminent, photos were serious.

The youth act like nothing can ever happen. Smiling, faking, the endless circus of corny distractions.

They are so woefully unprepared for hardship they'll drown in their toxins/fall by the wayside.

As political/economic freedom decreases, sexual freedom compensatingly increases. Aldous Huxley

PEOPLE PROBLEMS

Shocking stats: 70% of Christian men view porn regularly and the rest just sometimes, Lord help me!

Jesus said it's in the eyes: Porn is a form of adultery, something to despise.

Not just porn but flirts with clerks--so many marriage-debasing and adulterous actions by jerks

Any pastor who says he's gotta view smut to get it up is a liar, phony and adulterer/leave, STOP.

Shocked and hurt lady said: "I hate all his crap around, I hate him. I want him gone and his sin".

Wait for Jesus to turn it all around. He knows what's happening and will vindicate His own.

Shock, what to do: Reach out to friends and those who don't reply, END. Music/goin' on ahead.

Ontologically fatal insight: the world is not what you thought--your world has flip-flopped.

Now look ahead: far better than what you've had, a life of dread.

Champion, aspirer, discoverer, visionary, home and God lover, true patriot or pathetic piece of crap?

He's the slime ball, not you--but never go back to him though, just like you always do.

Give me power to go on Father cuz I sure don't feel like it. What a shock life is on a daily basis.

The SRI's blocked all pattern recognition so I continued to mess up without ever any correction.

PEOPLE PROBLEMS

All other women can't believe you took a stand. Now they'll all follow suit and make this demand.

I want honest, smart and enthused workers. Attention to detail, quick and inventive learners.

Maxine Watters is totally corrupt putting down Trump but the dumbed liberals eat it all up.

They're too dumb to understand it anyway.

A disgusting spirit coming into your house.

If they're gonna act that way don't let them in your house and it's your kids who are the worst.

Another silent empire is dirty jokes--a dark spirit, trains children, bad demonic hold, being yoked.

You should never allow off-color jokes in your home. Disgusting, dark, unhappy, demons.

Everything has gotta be upright, above board, clearly seen, understood, decent and straight.

Liberals are emotional wasteland--kill your spirit, misunderstand, make presumptuous demands.

it's an interactional process that takes place, as an ethologist I want to document that and be precise.

All I want is privacy, routine, beautiful surroundings to do my work now. A mansion on acreage with a wall.

There must be some nice decent men.

PEOPLE PROBLEMS

What made me change so fast? You said the buzzwords and that changed everything/it's a blast.

Man starts off as a potential genius and visionary only to end up a pedophile whoremonger.

Why does a pedophile look scruffy grunge? Cuz he couldn't care less, he's a predator not a sponge.

Mankind's plunge into wickedness.

He betrayed and lied to me but I don't feel bad cuz I got God my Dad.

What is a spongegrunge, it's a sinner with a double life, a manipulator and lecher too in style.

When things change the man may regress into porn--the most common problem of the hour.

These men are so low they don't mind the dark/dank and are just predators every day and hour.

Disgusting lechers are dying vultures.

Flesh-eating spirit: ravenous, rapacious, depthless, can't get enough (young women) or anything else.

Man is duplicitous cuz he has two sides. We all do (a matter of control) but crookedness is despised.

The false churches justifying gay marriage and abortion: compromisers with the world, I hate em.

He's lower than a dirty rat, he's a slug.

He's the dross, you're the most.

PEOPLE PROBLEMS

Two sides: With fear or trauma he regresses to previously successful strategies like tantrums.

The whoremonger does many things right but don't get sidetracked and stay in the light.

Is this the man who made not God his idol of devotion?

It's been a nightmare knowing you, living in a junk pile too.

Women think if they have to take it, I gotta take it and anything else they're not having it.

Male alcoholic insults, pulls her down, mocks her looks. What's there left but to just get drunk?

Once you see the light there is no reason to wait.

The lady said "I hate his guts so much it makes me wretch".

Alcohol Psychosis: a broken record. The same argument for 30 years and can't forget it, ever.

Broken record is never worked through. Incompleted mourning, distracting, avoiding the truth.

Reliance on unreliable people is a form of being unequally yoked and it makes one so provoked.

Here you're paying/relying on them but your spirit is vexed and it becomes a big mal-adaptation.

Computers level playing field so I'm on par with you--even broke someone comes along enthused.

In God's timing is there ever delay? No, even if a year or decade, trust Him ok.

PEOPLE PROBLEMS

You have developed something or a way of thinking that no one else has. It's called style: *panache.*

Needing workers desperately puts you in a sick relationship with them so relax/pray for wisdom.

Oh! I get it. Whenever they say they can do it it means they *can't* do it.

All new crew is good for you--no confusion from the past/ now you know just what you want, too.

No projections/resentments from the past, all new crew/more streamlined too, now success finds you.

You work hard all your life and then you retire. Now you can finally think, create and be inspired.

Is there ever delay in God's timing? NO, and that's what you gotta know.

Home: Unless I own it I gotta deal with people and I can't stand it.

Take failure as sign you're close, a cluster of em = you're right on the cusp and next to be blessed.

Humiliating failure today can bring your win as it pushes you to the end.

Utter humiliating failure was the kick in the butt you needed to get over the finish line undefeated.

She did me wrong but wasn't smart enough to see it so my correction brought a really big jolt.

You can't make them smart, so suddenly you may be alone--but God will always provide that one.

PEOPLE PROBLEMS

It's called decompensation after the shock of reality disintegration.

I see it as a mal-adaptation. Yes it's generated from within as genetic potential but rolls out with friction.

The genetic potential to devolve like that into total madness was incremental, in steps.

I didn't have the tools/wisdom to deal with it so just devolved without any control over any of it.

Stress = genetic symptoms roll out.

Even if they did know what you were talking about they don't care--so best to wait for someone rare.

Way out of poverty: Finish high school, keep a job for one year, don't have children until marriage.

Relax then a moment comes when you can't help but begin--then take it through to the end.

It's not you it's anyone who wrecks my concentration--it doesn't matter who it is, it's interruption.

The longer the break the more it all comes together when you get back.

Take more breaks, get away from it. Regroup, toke, look at view, adjust attitude = complete it, whew.

It's right brain or left. Too much focus--get receptive then reverse back into the locus/the best.

Why do you think too much work makes Johnny a dull boy? It's the left brain, it's boring, it annoys.

PEOPLE PROBLEMS

Man has imagination and higher brain to do far more damage than animals even lions or snakes.

Go right brain cornucopia then return to work--with holy spirit ease it completes it all/you're first.

It's been proven over and again: If my attitude is right the work completes in itself in a second.

There's a line and you don't cross it. If you do, suddenly everything goes twit.

People can be lower than animals due to sinful evil and total depravity, two main Christian principals.

Nip it in the bud, stay away. Lookout for attacks from envy and jealousy.

The greatest punishment for sin comes from peoples' subliminal and automatic rejection of evil.

He who fights with monsters should be careful lest he thereby become a monster. Nietzsche

He's lazy, careless and passive. You don't need this from this plastic poser keeping you captive.

Find porn on his computer he's a adulterer cuz Jesus says it's all in the eyes/but not to fear.

Men are emotionally brittle so heed my guides: Man views porn, woman rejects, he suicides.

Pornography is a silent toxic empire and if you're yoked to someone who's into it you've had it.

He has led you to believe you need him for protection but he's the one you need protection from.

PEOPLE PROBLEMS

It's a form of insanity: the effects of pornography. Not just yelling but mistakes, faux pas, profanity.

Pornography means he's comparing them to you! And some women don't care, don't become blue?

If someone loses money he's a loser. If he's a careless procrastinator it aggravates like a boozer.

He won't let you have any money but also loses it honey while insisting you waste money.

He's a waster and a loser. A waster IS a loser. Holes in his bucket, imposture.

Outside of discipline is self-indulgence and decay.

The trouble I had crawling out of my shell for all those years--total resistances and many tears.

No one understood me/I didn't understand myself but fortunately I found Jesus who fixed the mess.

You'll only feel comfortable out of that system completely--maybe you should recognize that, see.

Must forgive all you've ever known. They didn't know, they were as dumb as you before growth.

If those hormones mean yelling at your wife you don't put up with it--look beyond surface/feminists.

Men who check out women in public have no respect for their wives. The suffering is deep like knives.

This silent empire in men's lives must be shattered for good cuz it's about brain chemicals/selfhood.

PEOPLE PROBLEMS

After years of preparation you will finally cross the great divide. This is a sudden change--oh my!

You've done the work now get ready for "overnight" success tho' you've been workin' forever miss.

You work and work and suddenly the spotlight's on you and that's how it works so relax for perks.

The most inspired are also the most susceptible to captivation by demons so watch out friends.

You enable this kind a thing, you're just as bad as that cad.

Women are so desensitized/divorced from their feelings and bodies they don't even care.

Stop shame that stops your work. You gotta come out, it was just demons causing those quirks.

What we're talking about here is the effect of brain hormones and I have to adapt to those?

Online porn is a past-time of most men and the sign is yelling at their wives. Nip it in the bud, thrive.

No wonder marriages fall apart/start bickering with these subtle messages going on--that's porn.

If 70% of Christian men are into pornography, no wonder I don't wanna go to church--demons lurk.

Once you forgive em now you can take the good from the bad experience, get greater and go on.

PEOPLE PROBLEMS

Divine vindication is necessary for the relief of the saints. God gets the haters, since the ancients.

Bashed identity from apathy: lost steam, serenity and fascination with work God gave to thee.

Conservatives think like lions, liberals think like lambs.

Happy I never have to see you again. Tho' you robbed me I'm free to find new helpers and friends.

For that which is highly esteemed among men is abomination in the sight of God. Luke 16: 15

I don't care what it looks like, I believe that God is working.

You communicate thru a readily understandable image not by spouting off just to show your stuff.

It's about the copy not what I look like.

God loves seeing you fight the good fight, rejoicing and praising Him even when pricked by the knife.

I feel happy and free now I'm not unequally yoked to thee, it was terrible but now you're gone, whee!

I hated being dependent on you. You were dismissive, offputting, made me crazy too (so blue).

I can't walk with the wicked--the crooked, the double minded. Hooked to you was confinement.

Baby, the wicked like you with such poor character are easily recognized and they are everywhere.

PEOPLE PROBLEMS

Superior man can't be on the begging end cuz--unequally yoked--they will have power over him.

When interviewing workers you gotta use your intuition. This instinct will save you from destruction.

They just can't get it together, they can't see the whole. It's boring even trying, let God take control.

We want Christmas, Easter, town fairs and parades--it is sentimentality for the good ol' days.

Elder consciousness--saging--is more sedate, contemplative, pensive, creative and reclusive.

My function is to sit here 20 hours a day and do what I do while running the entire household too.

Rehabilitation: a leopard changing his spots?

I need solitude to bring it through.

He is now at a later stage in life, psychologically--more monastic, quieter, inward, universal.

You overcame so much, you went thru so much (God knows this) but after the pot is perfect it's over.

He uses your foes for discipline but when whole He turns on them worse so let that be the goal.

Remember it'll now be the opposite to all you known: fame not mocking, ridicule, rejection, scorn.

The past was just your lesson not life sentence so change your attitude to opportunities ahead.

PEOPLE PROBLEMS

Recalling past persecution takes you down to that location--like little anchors it pulls you down.

The person you knew at sixteen is not the same. It's another person so stop carrying that flame.

I'm not wasting time I'm regrouping and will be soaring.

Enjoy a walk, play ball with dogs, watch Bonanza, make some salsa, take a nap then watch the sunset.

The longer you wait the easier/faster it will complete.

It's "correct and firm" until the very end.

Don't work just get into that space where with holy spirit ease the whole thing completes itself: aced.

Deadlines are deadly so don't compulse just work on your receptivity to get it all done quickly.

Don't work--hold back strength--until that moment you cannot NOT work and you go to the end.

If you're just kind and attentive to animals you'll be amazed at the affection they will show you.

At last a coder who can replicate me the designer and I'm gonna party forever cuz he's so clever.

You'll never get a chance to tell me I'm doing it wrong/am a heretic cuz it's just Him and me: fantastic.

Open your perception to increasing opportunity in an abundant environment for you and me.

PEOPLE PROBLEMS

Cosmic: When finally whole (mature) everything comes into perfect order around the superior man.

Don't have to sell myself just read my words if you don't like em I don't care nor even know.

The mark of a brilliant teacher is how many don't come back.

To do your best work keep taking the day off. You will get so creative it will all finish itself.

This is for the delicate, the refined, the perspicacious, the fascinated, the sharp, the higher mind.

To do your best work just do what you want. You will want to work when sparked, that's my rant.

Don't come without calling. I don't like surprises cuz I have my own synchronicity/you ain't it.

I have nothing to brag about but daily assiduity and that's what brought me where I am today.

Every day even Sunday I arose at midnight and worked to the next night: a prepared mind is ready.

All sin creates insanity but with repentance the symptoms leave in a glorious return to normalcy.

Pornography has been minimized all this time but that's mainly liberals who debased us (slime).

Pornography a powerful yet unmentioned empire, a major focus, and it's hard to imagine this.

PEOPLE PROBLEMS

A rich life may be consolation for going to hell so don't envy prosperity or go under it's spell.

They know you/familiar with your habits. The bad ones make em hate you and the good won't make it up.

Why did it slip from consciousness? Because you adapted to it, no longer believe it or he denied it.

Women are coached to put up with this crap—pornography with men. That is bull my friends.

Porn is minimized by women—legitimized, justified, don't make waves, at least it's not a dame.

Christian forgiveness means to forget all the crap he did. It's what we came here to learn I guess.

I love hearing the crow in the morning and the crickets at night. I love my new home, outa the blight.

I don't do phones. I hate them with a passion and they give me headaches that last all day, ashen.

Phones are just a modern invention and people are obsessed with them: entry points for demons.

With email I can think about it/have a record of it, but phones are pure chaos and I'm thru with it.

Facetime, all that invasive stuff, it's none of your business what I look like, it's privacy vs. fluff.

Liberals think nothing of cutting corners constantly and they're corrupt—these aren't the old days, they're nuts.

PEOPLE PROBLEMS 2

More Trouble Than They're Worth

For every setback God has already arranged a comeback. Isn't God great? The divine Cure for sad sacks. What created that? Good is seen as bad and bad good and even the police will protect (and then release) the hood. Well now you're the ace taking great delight in spotting and putting creepy conformists in their place. Now you know how to spot em. You know their buzzwords that instantly peg em as scum. They think they're smarter than they are, even told they're intellectuals, a new breed/gold star. They already had a big head and now our coddling makes em ridiculously nervy (want us dead). All these decades they looked up to us, now they're here and are loving replacing us, full of sass. The white man is hated in every corner. This will not end well, it's the effect of Dunning-Kruger. They're using satanic hand signs (horns) and have no idea what it is or wouldn't care (like porn).

PEOPLE PROBLEMS 2

Good is seen as bad and bad good and even the police will protect (and then release) the hood.

They already had a big head and now our coddling makes em ridiculously nervy (want us dead).

All these decades they looked up to us, now they're here and are loving replacing us, full of sass.

The white man is hated in every corner. This will not end well, it's the effect of Dunning-Kruger.

They think they're smarter than they are, even told they're intellectuals, a new breed/gold star.

They're using satanic hand signs (horns) and have no idea what it is or wouldn't care (like porn).

Now you know how to spot em. You know their buzzwords that instantly peg em as scum.

You're the ace taking great delight in spotting and putting creepy conformists in their place.

It's busting through this screen--the resistance to genius in social cultures-- giving you sheen.

She slept with every man in town even husbands. We're not supposed to slut-shame just be fans.

Slut- and fat-shaming are necessary to save sick race but they've banned this cuz it's now all-ok.

It's too bad about him, he should love me though I'm fat and if not he's a misogynist sexist rat.

"I have sex with everyone but I'm a good person" she said--even bragged about it like Blanche did.

Don't argue, don't relate. You're higher, you know their game and their fate.

The effects of groups on consciousness: How fascinating as we learn that more is actually less.

It is catastrophic to be framed by people. Frame yourself or let God, simple.

No use being angry at em just see em as little children needing pablum so start today, tell em.

When they start up, don't go down that rabbit hole with them. Don't object or debate cuz you know em.

Viewing self against the ground of "them" you fall short but without em it perfectly hits the mark.

The result of being framed by them is shame or guilt but framed by God is infinity and depth.

You're absolutely inspired, what do you have to feel guilty about? That's from them, a black cloud.

Reason for fires in their words for y'all: California wants compact development to reduce sprawl.

California wants stack-housing to reduce sprawl and they also won't allow rural living for y'all.

The desktop Manual fits perfectly historically. It is hyper-synchronicity for this generation, truly.

PEOPLE PROBLEMS 2

We all know a good female role model. Just emulate her not the modern day rabble (they are awful).

Men, stop apologizing. It's pathetic you've been pushed this far but just repent and be uncompromising.

Speak for the heartbreak of your generation--like unconscious collective archetypes of man.

To get concealed carry, know how to shoot a pistol at short range and random killings are changed.

Just one person with concealed carry coulda saved twenty.

Scumbags like him are the reason for our 2nd amendment.

California burn plan will spread nationwide. They want us in city ghettos and not on the land.

The evil side of humanity plugging into high tech systems.

Wanna move em to the cities--that's why they're burning out Californians (even horses) on purpose.

Debauched and dirty 18th century England: the reaction *against* all that was the Puritans.

Are you the woman who publicly puts down her own father and her Savior?

What was so fascistic about it was how you enjoyed excluding me and I will never forget that.

Didn't wanna let me in cuz they'd have to change everything since I'm opposed to sinning.

It's hyper-synchronicity--it fits in history. You know what's happening, it's beyond evil thinking.

PEOPLE PROBLEMS 2

Which is worse: Hollywood or it's emulators? What about kin/friends acting like asinine imitators?

If they hate Trump or use buzzwords like "global warming" or like concepts, heed my warning.

Tho' they've done nothing, they deserve fame and fortune. That's the progressives but they're done.

Rule 1: Don't argue with em. Rule 2: Don't even think of em.

There's no way I'd ever grace their dumb liberal shows and argue with those who don't know.

And having to deal with *that*--are you kidding me? In your *home*?

"Likes" is no barometer of your value so get offa that thing

It's a progressive disease like anything else, but our constitution gives us freedom to do this.

Antifa is an adolescent group of idiots fighting with knives and bricks.

Remember how sick you were around em? Liberal climate does that so best to release em.

Sodomism means Homosexual supremacy.

HaHa a big fat cow preening on the red carpet. Isn't she marvelous this know nothing and a mess.

Don't start me on lesbians in the area--the most brazen and pugnacious group in America.

They've gotta hammer it in they're right--cuz inside they know they're wrong, saying bigots be gone.

By your attraction to the fake you've ruled out association with a most golden opportunity to take.

It's sickening: unnatural parings or anything else preposterous/erring, a depthless evil thing.

If they hate Trump, take joy! Now you know who to leave out or who will surely disappoint.

If someone loves Hillary, laugh it off. Back off, forget em: peanut galleries who mock and scoff.

I know you from your likes and will use that as a barometer to rid myself of you drippy hangers: yikes.

Just the fact you like that/think you're on the red carpet yet a TV addict but forget you, I fixed it.

Sickening isn't it, they could think like that? But that's the human tribe vs. God's men, His beloveds.

Since whole cultures go down together we must study social hypnotism the most--and it's here.

Women make fools of selves/show no power saying things like "my colleague, a nobel prize winner"...

Stand up/defend middle America not the leftist coasts, standing for wrong until they're toast.

Monsters on red carpet: jewels in a pig's snout.

They take you down cuz you are right and they are wrong.

We're sick of coastal liberals making decisions for us, the real.

I earned my independence from years of seeing what happens when you lose it.

How could you let these women take over like this? Nothing so much proves liberalism is false.

That's all there is out there: interconnecting realities fused together in a big hypnotic scare.

They are scary to clear minds: so dense, so heartless, so out of touch thinking they know much.

The culture-stealers have gone so far as to say we should feel proud for obesity or being slutty.

Things that would have meant a looney bin are now front and center as superior while we be enablin'

Canadians have had enough of Trudeau's leftwing ideology and he'll be gone to forestall a tragedy.

Men: you've gotta stop apologizing. Although so endearing it is all from social engineering.

Men you're gotta stop listening to crazy women or like Merkel a whole continent will fall to vermin.

Men: I know you want peace at any price, tranquility and sex so you tolerate feminist dogma, a hex

Copying a man's world of money wheeling/dealing, women are easily bought off--loyalty's not thought of.

What a great pleasure to live in this era where I can find out things 20 hours a day then tell ya.

PEOPLE PROBLEMS 2

Don't call it "new age" call it liberalism cuz conservatives restore the old paths for success/optimism.

America needs to be aligned with a Christian nation reforming itself: Russia.

It's so disgusting the coastal liberals' superficial sheen while inside, filthy things they believe in.

What an embarrassment these loser liberals about to fall. They aren't ready/don't know guns at all.

Putin sees Barrack and Hillary clearly and loves Trump. This man is our ally not our enemy hon'

As Obama/Clinton/Podesta go down people will see how it's evil Soros' globalist machinations.

Obama bought $65,000 hotdogs (boys) but you think Trump is bad (how liberal thinking disappoints).

They're as dumb as rocks but humans spout slogans by rote: no true smarts but it blocks ya know.

Coastal liberals see themselves as intellectuals. Can you believe that? We'll soon see you fools.

It is race discrimination to not want to hire criminals?

Without God they'll believe anything—any kooky rubbish demons think of.

Not Christian if they "love Jesus" the man/prophet but don't see Him as exclusive/they can't do that.

Americans are sinners too but somewhere still inside is the Christian work ethic that built this country.

Of course climate change exists but it's not man-made or to pay them carbon taxes.

It used to be the churches were for charity now government is as the churches become a rarity.

See the signs, nip it in the bud: that's a true leader like Trump.

They object to your correction then make the same darn mistake again.

It's horror dealing with zombies in charge of your nice life and things.

Due to the Dunning-Kruger effect of dummies thinking they're smart, if you correct them they object.

Computer warning: Don't waste time cuz you can get way out in left field, tangentialized.

In a chaotic era like ours people slip into weird archetypes and templates yet they can't see it.

Hillary does not love women if she's still married to a sexual predator and convicted rapist, vermin.

What if it were a child chained like that? I know it's a dog but they both have feelings/are sentient.

I used to be a feminist, even taught women's studies. I'm the opposite now after decades of curses.

They're for women--but love Hillary who's still married to a serial, convicted rapist/sadist.

He bit the victim's lip until it bled and that got her into bed but feminists love the Clintons instead.

PEOPLE PROBLEMS 2

It goes underground: she's happier but soon subconscious wisdom sets in and she's snippier.

What accounts for the hysterical female outburst? Sick cycles of denial vs. love, deceit vs. trust.

Weaker he is the more stripes come out cuz self-restraint takes strength and he's dropped out.

No psychiatrist can sort it out where lies and love co-exist. If he's in denial he's a liar and you're pist.

Your minimizing of sin (because it's prevalent) is so telling, but I'll forget it.

A womanizer's rehab: learning not to do it in front of her.

Eminem made a fool of himself at SNL--see what happens when you come against Trump the marvel?

I am sorry the tattoo will blur with age and look even dirtier. But you still must face it's not prettier.

Who are you to mark up the body God gave you. It's ugly, the bible says it's what the heathen do.

Does the wife ever think he's exhibiting for the nurses? No, it's always just an accident not sex curses.

Take hold of shield and buckler, and stand up for my help! Psalms 35: 2

For a couple hours I was terrified of his black and evil powers but I won't forget God will shower.

A zebra can't change it's stripes. He is what he is, there are bad seeds who are unsalvageable I guess.

What destroys marriages: sin. What repairs/makes good ones: repentance, starting all over again.

Bashing men when they're the ones who can protect them. Becoming less attractive, too easy giving in.

Becoming less attractive because he should love you anyway, but hey that's not the way to be lady.

If you don't be sweet lil' ladies, you'll be driven crazy or killed and you created the tragedy.

Ultimately all you can do is forgive then start again to live.

Love and abandon reality. Give that all up and then really see the sick relationship, a tragedy.

That devil is so dominating and peremptory too, I feel great peace every time I bid him adieu.

Share everything and make you feel guilty if you don't. It's all bull we're independent/this ain't God.

It's not just a white nationalist thing. Different but equal as everyone is happiest when separated.

Camille Paglia (famous feminist) is all for abortions, a heartless sadist or an intellectual, sis?

People cannot be equalized upwards so it means downwards, the lowest common denominator.

The hoax of black victimization and those who enable it. Colin Flaherty

Makes me sick you thinking I should accept that.

PEOPLE PROBLEMS 2

They wanna makes us in *their* image but then leave cuz it's a pig sty.

Equal but different/separate: otherwise it's conflict--like how you treat dogs--and we're sick of it.

The only cure for non-assimilation is a fifty year ban on immigration.

Ban newcomers and there is eventual assimilation of the others, or it's just more enclaves/no-goers.

Diversity is not only not our strength but completely destroys community cohesion. Robert Putnam

In London, knife crime is up 34% and 13,000 stabbings from invadees.

Christian children taken to Muslim foster homes.

Christianity faltered and was replaced by religion of equality (modernity) both political and economic.

Don't give me your false Christianity. We live in an age of prevalent pedophilia and it's all ok with ya?

Since a filthy sin is common we're supposed to accept it? Believe it or not, many pastors ignore it.

To so-called "pastors": Stop calling filthy sins of Satan a "sickness" then begin to heal as Christians.

Left is trying to sexualize children so they're conditioned to it. Like justifying pedophiles, think about it.

He was always into pornography calling it "German movies".

Pastors make it worse by condemning the scorned wife for her "hate" and saying he's just "sick".

Jesus was a real man taking on the temple of cheats. He didn't justify, comply or accept defeat.

The only freedom is freedom from illusion. Stefan Molyneux

You sound like the pope the way you justify this filth. What has happened to Christians/moral health?

Touching a child is as bad as penetration when it comes to tragic lifelong effects on the victim.

Saudis letting em date now but everything is above board not casual sex right away like here.

Immigration laws should benefit the people in the country, not those outside of it obviously.

If your enemy has a sword, get a bigger one. Christianity is not about being a wimp and laying down.

As smart as Milo is, he's indecent. Decency is our matrix, barometer and litmus test, amen.

Demographics is destiny but questioning government makes us a conspiracy theory.

People died so how dare you question the official story!

I'm not going to argue with some lawyer, just take the money you shyster--profession of poor character.

"Racism" is here defined: You care about your own race and you know that all races are different.

PEOPLE PROBLEMS 2

We're strong but also most fragile. We break, we go under but given the right fodder we go higher.

How much of the outsider can you tolerate? That is the breaking point.

Whites have been told they don't even exist, why protect what is theirs?

Women have played a major role in the migrant crisis in Europe--more xenophilic and emotional.

White self-interest is not racism: accepting all groups have interests fosters mutual understanding.

EcoScience final assault: depopulate the planet by confusing gender and putting chemicals in food/water.

Blacks were highminded and creative: look at Soul Train! Then MTV made em thugs/into drugs.

This was all subversion thru entertainment and we were all part of it--now thugs top the grammy list!

Bad boys and bad girls are sick freaks but actually have very high self-esteem, billionaires it seems.

I was unequally yoked to an ex-Obama intern posing as a virtual assistant, can you believe that?

They can sexualize infants--Kinsey proved that in the sixties. A longterm plan, Lord come please.

Making kids non-gender is part of a UN plan to depopulate the planet, for decades we've known it.

Is it a boy or a girl? Let the state and it's programming decide, not you.

PEOPLE PROBLEMS 2

America has become coarse, pornographic, anti-man--it all goes together cuz women hold the line.

Disney caught in shocking sexualization of babies, not even infants, and you love liberals/Hillary?

Don't forget how brilliant these founders were, kept us free all that time. But now there is unholy swine.

Women are largely shallow/can't see what they're doing to me, you, the whole world/no more free.

They think they're being nice and loving and are so blind they can't see the destructive people-flooding.

Virtue-signaling and liberalism is so obviously a mental illness and I don't see how we can last.

Women are rabid sloganizers but to them peer acceptance is more important than *what* ideas.

Women: they got us into this mess and are still getting us into it--will real men come forward, please?

Just the fact peer approval is more important than *what* ideas show's where women are at, geez

The sexualization of babies is truly the next level of depravity from Disney.

Their first word is not "mama" or "papa" but "smash the patriarchy".

Watch out for leaks to the street. Whether gossip-called-concern or social manipulators do speak.

It wasn't "Sheila" it's that most women are like Sheila and the morals she lacked.

PEOPLE PROBLEMS 2

No one wants to hear about the huge differences between genders/races--to liberals they're all aces.

Boys not doing well in school, males seen as bad, men live shorter lives, wives snipe, mock, despise.

Son, what must you do to be a man? "I have no clue, no guidelines, no rules, masters nor scripts".

Be ladies & gentlemen not groveling supine minions.

The dumb tend to be social--the smart don't have time, finding it silly cuz they've got goals.

God said we'd be despised, put aside, walked on by, framed by those who lied, on the wrong side.

The dumber they are the more social. I always thought so, I'd so prefer to be creative all alone.

The dumb are much more social cuz what else do they have but yak-yak-yak or they'd go mad.

There's only two ways to fix things in life: the club (force) or your words. Stefan Molyneux

Lady found the compromised church boring and social and the gentleman said he'd never again go.

And to think we hated all that syrupy sentimentality, after going thru this we want it all back, truly.

I have no children--will leave my fortune to saving dogs from Asian dog-meat operations.

When you're expected to socialize and everyone wears a disguise/spouts lies, impossible guys.

You believe that crap cuz that's what you learned in school. Not your thoughts--it's a plan, subliminal.

Sorry I can't be interrupted. I can't let you determine my day and this lesson I learned the hard way.

Full of bitterness and captive to sin.

It took years to recover from a feminist tyrant over me and when I saw her later she was an old lady.

Ku Klux Klan mentality on the left is what we have today. They own it all including what we say.

Bedlam's occurring in CA cities. They've got the green light now, they can do anything and stay free.

Sanctuary cities are smugglers and criminal aliens best friend.

Where is great compassion of liberals in Frisco? There isn't any--liberalism is just a front ya know.

Life/death of a sea lion is worth more than a white woman in Frisco today: year in jail and big fine, ok?

Tried by a jury of his peers--you mean felons and illegal aliens? Death is near for many Californians.

Liberal newspapers like L.A. Times didn't even report on this. Shocking as lemmings approach the abyss.

Matt Lauer and friends are fake news gatekeepers of lies, distracting you with foolish disguise.

PEOPLE PROBLEMS 2

Why do women support/condone criminals? Same reason they love bad boys tho' it's subliminal.

I'm done with bad boys, there's no attraction there. I like decency in a man and it's so darn rare.

Politics is downstream from culture (coarse, pornographic, anti-man) so we've lost protection.

We love Trump's unpresidentialness.

Women were ok and splendid when sweet lil' ladies but now they're the worst: debauched and shady.

Do not visit San Francisco, see? Cuz if you're mugged, robbed or shot the killer will go free.

Brad Pitt drank cuz he left his first wife. You ensnared him sexually then he felt guilt, shame, strife.

A woman meets another woman, sizes her up and puts her in her place. All thru history that is the case.

Democrats love Lena Dunham who said she wanted to carry a baby so she could abort for "solidarity".

Those who support sanctuary cities are to blame for the death of Kate Steinle. Sean Hannity

Lena Dunham's idea of feminism was to steal car keys and not give a bleep what her father thinks.

As a boomer who cut corners it was a shock as he went by-the-book on everything, but it took.

They made us hate America and some even changed their names. It was a set-up: we were framed.

PEOPLE PROBLEMS 2

World's worse dictatorships always had an image of benevolence followed by death and hardship.

They made us think nothing of illicit sex but after restoring the old paths we see them as the best.

Don't let em go out unchaperoned. You can't trust anyone and it would be better to be alone.

Don't let your girls out with boys or groups, cuz if they insist on chastity they'll be called fools--true?

It takes rare strength at 16 to go against group's thinking so I'd chaperone and be called crazy.

Satan (and his people) are jealous of God (and His people) so we gotta get hep, fence up, be real.

They read whatever agrees with them then think "everything is fine" when it isn't, they could die.

A self-righteous hack politicizing a tragic death.

Ego blinds so it's easy to use events to grandstand but I'd use restraint to save embarrassment.

She's a self-righteous hack politicizing a tragic death--that's what she was grandstanding like that.

Elites aren't being pushed out of neighborhoods by immigrants so they have "blissful ignorance.".

Having fled from foreigners to do the job I found the Americans were lazy, sleepy, inattentive slobs.

PEOPLE PROBLEMS 2

When you finally find one you can work with (energy), treat him like gold cuz the rest is lunacy.

When you finally find one reliable after going thru the dregs you feel you've won the lottery, it's sick.

Women encouraged to lie about him, do him in, make him pay/suffer, take away his children (vindication).

Sarah Sanders is taking down the press every day like a boss.

We can keep our farms--no estate tax for farmers! For America, Donald Trump is the savior.

As things fail like in California, people fall more into sin I tell ya--then divorces rise in America.

Tho' they do it all wrong still they may hang on but you must fire, avoid, block, take a rest, sing a song.

Your worst enemies will encourage you to do wrong--those "friends" from the liberal throng.

Ben Afflect the liberal pest had ancestors who were slaveowners.

A crazy liberal woman with way too much power. Women are the reason for the mess we're in, wow.

Why so much perversion and sex harassment? Cuza women acting like that, an embarrassment.

Chinese owns California and that's why the fires. They have it planned but it's just business of liars.

You go to California to get poor and you leave to get rich.

PEOPLE PROBLEMS 2

Liberals are syrupy fake nice but wait a minute you'll see their vice.

The ugly, old, washed out Barrack staying relevant with this silly dumbed youth base: "I love rock".

So reckless with my money but so stingy with his own. In those cases it's better being alone.

Men arrested in hospitals for exposing themselves to nurses--they're falling into sick sex curses.

Globalists call liberty movement a fake, fraud, won't deliver but it's the third world in culture wars.

Tyrants and parasites: The left aborts more than half of black children and sexualizes kids too.

Hospital flash: surrounded by young flesh pedophiles can't resist since hospital gowns = easy access.

It's the spirit inside doing the flashing (exhibiting). It's natural for it to do these things.

Martin Luther King is now bad (removed) since he didn't mention LBGTQ tho' it didn't exist then.

Obamacare is legislation by laxative. Greg Gutfeld

Cultural Marxism was the translation from the have/have nots to the oppressors and the oppressed.

"Haves vs. have-nots" didn't work in America so Marxists switched to "racism" during Obama.

PEOPLE PROBLEMS 2

The secret of their influence: the liberal intelligencia pay no price for being wrong (think of that).

If there's a price for being wrong they'd have to think about it, change their ways or be eliminated--not.

Conservatives aren't flawed, they're pragmatic.

The accusation of racism has made small towns devoid of any meaning. Douglas Murray

Intellectuals give people handicapped by poverty a further handicap of victimhood, a real tragedy.

Hollywood dames dress in black but it was liberal buddies doing the groping and this will come back.

The liberal phonies dressed in black can't win cuz it's a setup job--another empty try--but we have God.

The defunct pope lets bare-breasted women feed in sanctuary but it's all ok don't you think, hehe.

Liberals: Do you know what open borders does to dogs? Do you ever think of that, let alone God?

Our dear Trump is getting more audacious and sure of himself every day and I'm so proud, say Hurray!

Whenever he talks of all the starving children in the world you know he's a liberal cuz we can't help that.

Every democrat in congress voted against tax cuts for the American farmer-- can they get any meaner?

PEOPLE PROBLEMS 2

 **Farm country is God's country. Donald Trump**

If the democrats had their way they'd reinstate every regulation that's killing us vs. the POTUS.

Not a word about Islamacists killing females--she backs these oppressors but attacks American males.

America's the best place for women but she grandstands so you won't see what a witch she is, man!

If you see em on TV watch their hands by which they always pay homage to the devil's fans.

Why are our American men homeless? Because they can't trade lodging for sex. Stefan Molyneux

Women: It's not that all men are bad but that you chose the wrong man.

On the right, government exists to keep your freedoms but on the left it exists to buy your vote.

We love watching Di Nero do himself in. We love it when you "intellectuals" act like 13-year olds.

The star's $400 shirt read "poverty is sexist".

Swollen corrupt satanic Hollywood.

Queen sees through Meghan, a liberal leftist snowflake who hates Trump and everything decent.

How is she indecent? She wants open borders so we're raped/robbed, effecting our descendants.

Liberals are against Iranian protests by wonderful smart people held down for decades--aren't libs great.

PEOPLE PROBLEMS 2

All they care about is mean tweets and misgendering people, not about the present widespread evil.

Left says we must punish whites for the past. It's due compensation tho' they're innocent/miscast.

Just cuz it's a trendy topic doesn't make it right. Just cuz it's common doesn't make it legitimized.

Whenever someone says "I'm not trying to screw you" you know he's trying to screw you.

Who's doing all the groping? It's liberals loved by millennials tho' they protest it's all men, what fools.

So sorry to cut into your social life with the other hags on the red carpet bragging like they've made it.

Whoopi says Trump is the Taliban cuz he won't pay for her contraceptives: how ridiculous.

Sadiq Khan has the tranny toilets running but couldn't care less about acid attacks or stabbings.

Gay clubs are fast tracks into homo lifestyle and cruising with adults the vile in this trendy sin in style.

Bad men exist, bad women exist. That doesn't mean all men are bad except to the feminist.

Has embracing left wing politics been bad for the church? Membership collapsed, left em in a lurch.

We need to be re-horrified by homosexuality. Linda Harvey

All through human history homosexuality explodes right before destruction as it brings it on.

PEOPLE PROBLEMS 2

What I saw all around was an emboldened lowlife criminal class dominating small California towns.

California a democrat sanctuary state reflected in debauchery, disrespect, homelessness and trash.

Everything starts in California which I escaped. Hopeless, homeless, trashed, dreams dashed.

In one desert town a gang of teen thugs took over and the cops wouldn't do a thing to these jokers.

Californians are satiated, coerced and sedated into accepting a lower and lower third world state.

"Non-violent" crimes in California: Holding an elderly hostage or raping while drunk--that's just a few bud.

California is a sanctuary state, meaning: it harbors criminals.

Outa California for two years and I'm still edgy, looking over my shoulder--no way to live when older.

California is a shithole too Donald.

In California I was put down, regulated and edgy but here I've got a salon, known for my abilities.

Inner-city criminals spreading out thru small towns who are not equipped to handle this behavior.

As small towns fall hostage to ne're-do-wells there are no repercussions except going to hell.

The naughty boys at fake news love saying "shit hole" all day--360 times, ok?

Breaking thru delusion is hard with a child being taught--it's the same with all the lies they bought.

Ethno-Nationalism is shared heritage, language, faith, and ethnic ancestry vs. destruction/tyranny.

To solve race problems we can't just chant slogans which are coo coo and wrong.

Your politicians are putting a bunch of dumbass, entitled, evil or illiterate people over you: watch.

That's why they cry, rant and rave. They bought the lies from school starting with the first grade.

While we're all sinners God has put in us a holy hatred for it in all it's forms and thus we're winners.

They attack Christians cuz they don't get angry--until they do. Stefan Molyneux

Libs said they'd leave if Trump wins so why not move to Haiti, friends?

Little children at CNN love saying a dirty word on TV and getting away with it but we see thru them.

So the little boys got to say the word "shit" all day and pin it on the president, what a trip.

The liberals care so much about Haiti but not the millions raised for it then stolen by Hillary?

Even tho' they say sh*t 10X a day they blow this up instead of the *real* issues which require study.

PEOPLE PROBLEMS 2

I read between the lines, i see tell tale signs. Women are more intuitive than men at all times.

He'd like to shove it onto you as a paranoid psychotic cuz you see the light.

Look at what he's already done, not how he seems--his false image/facade--to stay on the beam.

People are just evil but it's covered over so it doesn't seem real. Track record, that's how you tell.

Wickedness is man's default setting. You gotta be strong to restrain.

You abandoned yourselves to soft prodigal living and to the pleasures of self-indulgence. James 1:5

You have fattened your hearts in a day of slaughter. James 1:5

Whites are bad when they leave (white flight) and bad when they come back (gentrification of blacks).

Arrogance of narcissistic criminals brings them down. Boldness brings success, then the mess.

Fake victim hoaxes mean instant fame and tremendous sympathy for the instigator who is lying.

Like a dog to his vomit he went right back to it: that's the sensual devil as the bible describes it.

They call Trump "crude" cuz he doesn't have a shiny veneer as we're oh so eloquently screwed.

Due to rampant pornography and pedophilia the barbarians line up on the periphery I'll betcha.

PEOPLE PROBLEMS 2

Libs steeped in ridiculous egalitarian notions will switch when pilloried for speaking obvious truths.

It's 40 X more likely for a black to assault whites than the other way around, yet they're told to fight.

"Freedom Acts" etc. are always the opposite: If they incarcerate you they "free everyone else".

They get us all worked up for justice then nothing happens--it all fizzles out. Will they ever arrest the cabal?

He's articulate in left wing ideology but if he loses swings to bad language and attacking the winner.

Never argue with idiots. They will drag you down to their level and beat you with experience. Mark Twain

Eminem sobbing and crying: "It should have been Hillary...wha wha wha wha".

Eminem calls Trump a "f**king turd" because turds prefer turds.

To all you sister wives: I can't even stand to share my man's mind.

The last thing I need is false Christian/liberal female trivializing this or telling me to accept it.

To the woman on facebook wearing the thong: get a life, write a book, sing a song.

They are the "spirit of right and good" and everything else must "bow to their presence".

You act like you need the approval of your silly generation--can't you broaden?

PEOPLE PROBLEMS 2

The evil are out there deceiving playing the victim role so you believe em and into hell following them.

Do not fall for it: these wicked women and their empty sayings.

Our country was hijacked by fools and traitors destroying our culture.

Scientific revolutions take place one funeral after another. Anonymous

These are no-good people for the things they believe in, evil. Who'd wanna listen with no appeal?

And what of the men involved with feminist slime: weak and pathetic girlie men not worth a dime.

Everyone suffers with divorce. The men horribly, kids, pets! All due to this globalist plan, a curse.

Blacks like Oprah/Obama talk like preachers to emotionalize and brainwash you to be controlled.

Smart blacks stand out and don't like em any better than we do so when hearing the facts: whew.

Who has time to worry about ISIS terrorists when gender pronouns are being disrespected?

Having been taught debauchery and acting on it, seared consciences just can't accept God.

To broadcast his virtue signaling of tolerance while at the expense of competence was the worst.

You can take Oprah outa the ghetto but not the ghetto outa Oprah. --Oprah's mother.

KAREN KELLOCK BOOKS:

AFFINITY OR MISERY
AGELESS CORNUCOPIA
AMERICA AWAKE!
AMERICA'S DAFT ERA
ARTS OF PALEO FASTING
AUTOPHAGY ON CHEATERS
BACKSTABBING NEUROTICS
BETRAYAL TRAUMA
BOOMERS AND BROKENNESS
BOOT ON NECK
CHAMPION GUIDES
COMMIE NUTHOUSE
COMMIES
COMMUNIST SPIRIT
CONTAGION OF MADNESS
CONTAGIOUS MADNESS
CULTURE CLASH BASHED
DAFT LEFT
DAILY FASTARIAN
DAM RATS
DIVERSITY IS CRUELTY
E-RACE WHITE
THE END OR A BEND?
FEMALE BULLIES AND FEMI-NAZIS
FEMALE CARNALITY
FEMALE DUMB DOWN
FEMINISM AND RUIN 1 & 2
FIX FOR MISFITS
FOOLS & TRAMPS
FREEDOM SPEAKING
FRENEMY ENABLER
FRENEMY LIAR
FRENEMY THIEF
FRENEMY TRAITOR
TRENEMY TYRANT
GENIUS IS HELD DOWN
GLOBALISLAM
GOD USES THE FLAWED
HAZE OF THE LATTER DAYS

THE HERD IN WORDS
HIX POLITIX
HOW THEY RUINED US
JUST SKIP DINNER
LE FEMME AND THE COMMUNIST SPIRIT
LIBERAL CHAOS & ROT
LIBERAL DOUBLETHINK
LIBERAL GALL 1 & 2
LIBERAL SHOVE-DOWNS
LOCK YOUR GATE
MANUAL FOR SUPERIOR MEN
MODERN ART FROM HELL
MOSTLY FAKE
NOTES TO CHAMPS 1 & 2
OVERCOME FRENEMIES
PC MAKES US CRAZY
PEOPLE ARE CRUEL
PEOPLE PROBLEMS 1 & 2
PERSECUTED GENIUIS
POLI-PSYCH MYSTERIES
PRETENTIOUS SLOBS
QUEEN BEE
RETURNING TO FIRST NATURE
THE SCHOOLS SCREWED EM UP
SEASON OF TREASON
SEPARATE MEANS HOLY
SOCIAL HYPNOTISM
SOLITUDE SOLUTION
SUPERCILIOUS
TOAD TO PRINCE
TRIALS CYCLES
TRUMP VS. GROUP
TRUST IN TRASH
THE TRUTH ABOUT PEOPLE
UNDERHEANDEDLY CLEVER
WALK TALL WITHIN WALLS
WE'RE NOT ALL ONE
WINNERS SKIP DINNER
WORK OR SMERK

KAREN KELLOCK PH.D.

M.S. Political Science, San Diego State. Ph.D. in Psychology, University of California Irvine. Postdoctoral: UCI School of Medicine, Dept. of Psychiatry [NIMH Grants]. Developed the Debris Theory of Disease, a theory of system pathology in 120 books and 22 textbooks for the general public. The theory has a general formula: All disease is obstruction, all recovery is elimination, all success is attraction. The three obstructions are people, habit and food. Remove obstruction and snap to your goals, waiting in the wings.